RODNEY SEAGULL

Chips, Ice cream and Cake

Written by
Trudy Davidson

Illustrated by
Pei Jen

Rhyming Moments

For Bethany
To our sweet, clever and talented entertainer. You are a joy to watch.

www.rhymingmoments.co.uk
First published 2022 by Rhyming Moments Books
61 Bridge Street, Kington HR5 3DJ

ISBN – 9781739121716

Text copyright Trudy Davidson 2022
Illustrations copyright Pei Jen 2022
The rights of Trudy Davidson and Pei Jen to be
identified as the author and illustrator of this work
has been asserted in accordance with the
Copyright, Designs and Patents Act 1988.

A CIP catalogue for this book is
Available from the British Library upon request.

RODNEY SEAGULL

Chips, Ice cream and Cake

Written by
Trudy Davidson

Illustrated by
Pei Jen

Chips, ice cream and cake...
Everywhere!

It is all too much for Rodney Seagull
- Treats are all he can see.
So excited - his face full of glee.

Rodney **Swoops,**

glides

and

soars,

Heading towards the shore.
Down, down - as fast as he could dive!
He feels so free. So alive.

Chips, ice cream and cake.
Getting closer!

The food is not far from hungry Rodney.
Tasty treats his beak can't wait to eat.
So excited he starts to wiggle his feet.

Plunging,

Sailing

and twirling around,

Rodney can see the sandy ground.

Dive, dive, hover and swoop.

Rodney does a loop the loop.

Chips, ice cream or cake.
Which first?

Swoop - Rodney aims for a cone.
A hand appears...
Stop...He flies up alone.

Dive - Rodney aims for a chip.
He doesn't make it...

Stop...
He meets a toy ship.

Plunge - he aims for some cake.
A hat appears...

Stop...
He puts on the brake.

Rodney begins to screech and squawk.
As he lands upon the sidewalk.

A lady stops and says, "How sweet!"
Chips are thrown at Rodney's feet.

Rodney laughs and gives a squeal -
He quickly eats his yummy meal.

Rodney gives a hoot and coo.
A man stops and says, "Clever you!"
Ice cream lands on the path –
Rodney gives a satisfied laugh.

Rodney starts to croon and cry.
A lady stops and says, "Talented guy!"
Cake is offered to his beak.
Rodney fills each cheek.

chips,

ice cream

or cake.

No more!
Rodney's tummy was full and round,
as he rested on the ground.

Happy and full, Rodney sat and thought,
an important lesson he had just been taught.

No longer would he dive to steal.
Instead, he would sing and earn his tasty meal.

Rodney swoops, gliding back to his nest.
He was ready to have a jolly good rest.

Sweet dreams Rodney.